The Young Actor's Notebook
by
Dennis Hilton-Reid

ISBN: 1548367524
ISBN-13: 978-1548367527

DEDICATION

To Mary. Thru Thick n' Thin

This book isn't to be read as a text book or a how to book.
This is not a book about technique or process.
I refer to the work as a rehearsal, teacher as director.
You don't need to read this book all in one sitting, you can
read a sentence one day, a Mantra the next. There is no
order to how you read it. Keep it in your back pocket,
carry it with you everywhere you go.
Consult it when in need.
This book is about the inner thoughts of your creative life.

This book is about you, for you.

Let go into the nothingness.

Are you afraid of being seen?

Class Vs. Rehearsal.

What are you wearing to class today?

Shorts, flip flops, a fancy skirt, a pair of trendy jeans, expensive sneakers?

Are you ready to roll on the floor, play, jump up and down, bounce against a wall, sweat and let the funk roll off **you?**
If you're dressed for a party, dinner party, dance party or an Arty Party then rethink what you're wearing, because you're not ready to work.

If you're in rehearsal dressed for Fashion week, then you're in the wrong business.

Choose your work clothes carefully.

Would you want to see your dentist wearing a Darth Vader Mask?

Be smart, be a worker amongst workers, let your talent show, not your haute couture.

Simple guidelines on rehearsal space etiquette: where rehearsal and class differ, and moving into action.

First of all, rehearsal is not class, class is not rehearsal is not class is not rehearsal.

Difference #1: Technique must be turned into action, therefore in rehearsal you have to shape your work toward performance.

Difference#2: Once you walk into the rehearsal room start **warming up.** It's your responsibility, no one is going to tell you to do this.

Difference # 3: Write down your own blocking as you work staging. Yes you have a Stage Manager, however doing this for yourself helps you learn your lines quicker, as the **act of notation** endows and deepens the work.

Difference #4: Never underestimate the power of note taking.

Difference #5. No eating during rhsl, only water.

Difference #6 Have you turned off your cell phone? Is your focus more on your phone than on your work? There is more to learn in the room than there is on Social media. Also the phone is another way of shutting down, isolating, being unavailable and giving into your fear.

Are you listening to your Director…I mean really **listening?**

Are you giving 100%?

Rehearsal is a different animal, with different requirements: It is the place to try out all possibilities and be willing to crash and recover, crash and recover, over and over again. Rehearsal is and is not about exploration, rehearsal is and is not about your demand for results.

Rehearsal is about your technique, your ability to sustain, putting all into practice. When the resident doctor graduates from the classroom to the floor of the ward, they are expected to have the understanding and grasp of medical theories and the ability to put that knowledge into the practicum of action. That's what you should expect from yourself, you, the Actor.

When you move into the rehearsal studio, put technique into action, action into impulse, impulse toward crafting your performance.

Dennis Hilton-Reid

Thoughts

We keep on digging deeper inside, we may never get there, but we keep on digging never the less.

The 8 points of the rehearsal Octagon:

1. ### Concentration and Physical Well Being.:

   Why you may ask (even if you didn't I'll tell you anyway) is concentration and physical well being in the same category? The preparatory work of the actor can get intense, stressful and exhausting as it is exciting and exhilarating, so we need to take care of ourselves; we are own barometer.
   If you're sick, feeling faint, dizzy, then you have to tell someone, it's not the Army, we don't march till we drop. Be smart, make healthy choices.

Quick simple steps to check for loss of concentration.

(a) are you hydrated?

(b) are you having a blood sugar rush? If so take the appropriate action.

(c) Are you feeling sleepy? Breathe, stretch the legs and arms, stand up, get the body moving.

2. ### Focus

Be a copious note taker.

Always have a notebook and pen out and ready.

3. ### Asking Questions:

Don't be afraid to ask a question that someone else has already asked, try using the "Just to clarify" qualifier.

4.   Being Prepared:

Know your lines; know your blocking; wear pieces of clothing your character would wear.

5.   Make a Decision To:

(a)   Make a choice
(b)   Be willing
(c)   Take a risk

6.   To Play

Be available to do whatever your director throws at you without questioning.

7.   To Speak Up

Do you have an idea that could help the scene, fix a scene that is stumping the Director? Don't walk home thinking, "I should have said that."

Ask the question **after** the experience, for then you are coming from a more informed place.

Dennis Hilton-Reid

A Play is like a murder mystery, you just have to follow the clues

MANTRA #1.

The Actor must always be in the State of Play. If you're not in a state of play you cannot create anything.

"You have to be in a state of play to design. If you're not in a state play, you cannot make anything."

-Paula Scher

"Work is just serious play."

-Saul Bass.

Confusion:

What is confusion?...*the state of being bewildered or unclear in one's mind about something: she looked about her in confusion.*

The Actor cannot afford to be confused not for a second. Because after that, you're lost in the hallway of confusion, that leads you to the room of regret, toward the no stairs stairwell of spiraling insecurity to the infinite pit of self hatred.

Confusion for the Actor is dangerous, it reminds me of the famous novel by Chester Himes, "Blind Man with a Pistol" A blind man with pistol is dangerous because he doesn't know what he's aiming at.

"What started it?"
"A blind man with a pistol."
"That don't make sense."
"Sure don't."

Head Games:
(also known as the Actors Death Grip)

The Actor's brain is a minefield of traps that result in the endless swirl of feelings of frailty and fragility.

If you can identify the thought and feeling then you can combat and defeat it.

If you play Head Games with yourself then read on...

Head Games is the moment when your mind takes over like a car with no driver.

The Actors mind is a runaway car.

The Head Games can start before you go on stage. The rata tat tat of the maniacal machine gun motor mouth of negativismo.

When the Death Grip of the heebie-jeebies hits the moment you step on stage, or worse when you're in the middle of a scene, what do you do? How do you thwart the thoughts of self-doubt, the crippling voices of chaos, the flurry of flashing images of uncertainty, cueing in the optimal center of the brain?

The list of endless feelings of frailty that end up in timidity include:

1. Judging self

2. Watching self

3. Insecure, unsure

4. Self-critiquing performance

5. Observing self

So, the question is, how do you handle the voices?

First, recognize them, hear them, separate them,
acknowledge them, **then let them go**. Do not **deny**
them, never deny the thoughts, just accept them.
Once you **accept** them, then you can use them.
Everything is recyclable, as the thought enters for a reason.
Through practice you can turn the thought into action
since the thoughts are always the same, and they usually
pop up like a recurring dream.

Now we have to look at the basis of the Head Game and
where it emanates from, and that place is Fear.

Fear:

Take your pick.

    a.   *an unpleasant emotion caused by the belief that someone or something is dangerous, likely to cause pain.*

    b.   *a feeling of anxiety concerning the outcome of something or the safety and well-being of someone:*

F.E.A.R. aka: Fuck Everything And Run or False Events Appearing Real.

If we believe what we are told, fear is the basis for everything. It represents our raw, primal feelings. The fear of not getting what we want and the fear of having it taken away because fundamentally, we all just want to be loved.

So, how do you know when you are in fear?

What are the signs?

- Reacting to a critique.
- Being defensive.
- Attacking someone else.
- Wasting time.
- Judging someone else's work.
- Gossip.
- Self pity.
- Seeking attention (being needy).
- Being disruptive.

And this is where some self-analysis is required, as an Actor you should have a keen sense of self-awareness, you must know thyself.

Embrace Your Fear.

Fear as a positive feeling: fear drives us to create, to eat, to survive, to be heard, to be seen.

Thoughts

The No No's! Of what to do when in Rehearsal:

Navigate and negotiation.

Never ask the Director how you're doing, it sounds desperate and there's nothing more off putting than a desperate actor.

Never answer for another actor, it causes resentment.

Unsolicited advice is never wanted, unless sought out.

Never give suggestions to another actor.

The question is why isn't your focus on your text analysis, beats, subtext, actions, objectives.

Have you made any choices, are you thinking about choices to make?

Have you come into rehearsal with a game plan, a working plan of ideas, are you just ready to work?

Professionalism:

Can you work with others? Let go of all personal feelings, because in this moment in rehearsal, it's not important. Being a professional means: leave your personal business, likes, dislikes, deaths, marriages and divorces, outside of the door, as well as the personalities.

Always choose Principles before Personalities.

Performance fear: the visceral.

Voice is tight, no air, cannot breathe, mouth is dry, feel dizzy, having an out of body experience, want to sleep, want to run away, NOW!
Hate acting, hate the theatre, why did I choose to do this to myself?
Ha! Fuck the audience! Shit my parents are out there, are they going to think I'm____? Maybe I am a fraud and I've been fooling myself.
Oh no! I don't remember my first line.

What to do? Embrace it, every word. Make every thought a self diagnostic review- every fear based negative, review, each lie and check it against the truth, which is "I'm prepared and ready."

If you're having a bad rehearsal/day, stop and start all over again.

e.g. It's twelve forty p.m. and nothing is going right, then you make a decision that at one o'clock you're going to start your day all over again.

At the end of the rehearsal day, take an inventory.
Find a quiet space and run through the positives and negatives.

Chances taken, chances missed; where was the growth and where were the missteps, and is there a plan of action for the next day.

Rehearsal is about opportunity.

Most important, what did you contribute today?

MANTRA #2

.

"Feelings are not facts, but it's a fact that we feel."

-Anon.

The Inspired Moment:

I was sitting in the orchestra seats watching a well known actor perform in a Tony award winning Broadway play one night. Half way through the second act there was a set change. The actor playing one of the leads came out and waited as the mechanical Broadway set appeared-I, along with rest of the audience, was engrossed in the action- the actor stood there waiting for the set as it slowly sneaked out, and he waited and waited, as we waited and waited; the set cranked to a halt, slightly camouflaged by the darkened upstage. The actor stood there for a few seconds but what I'm sure to him seemed like twenty-four interminable hours. So, what did he do? He walked offstage and waited for the stage hands to fix the problem. This man is a great actor, his work in the play is memorable, strong, powerful and risk taking.
Yet he missed the Inspired Moment.

A friend of mine recounted an experience he had while watching a play in L.A.:

It was a Murder Mystery-a whodunit. And as with any good whodunit, the murderer isn't revealed until the end. The play opens Act 1 Scene 1, an actor goes up on his lines and jumps to the last act, to who actually did it! And with two hours left to go- now what? The cast seized the moment and reworked the whole play from that point back to the beginning.

That's an Inspired Moment.

These are examples of the Inspired Moment - you either take the moment that's presented to you or you don't. The actor who doesn't go with the Inspired Moment isn't playing the truth in front of them, which is the opportunity of taking change and impulse into action, to create, explore, running head first into danger laying waste to fear. The Inspired Moment is when the unexpected happens, as it will and often does in live theatre.

The missing cue, missing prop, missing actor...

Do you freeze?

Or...

Do you make a decision to grab the Inspired Moment?

MANTRA #3.

Just Say Yes.

Art is created in the sub-conscious.

The sub-conscious: concerning the part of the mind of which one is not fully aware but which influences one's actions and feelings.

Athletes, Musicians, Yogis, Martial Artists, Healing Practitioners all tap into the sub conscious. It's the area lying below our conscious self that is vast and open, power infinitesimal just waiting to be harnessed.

In Martial Arts the sub-conscious slows everything down, movement and time become your friend, so you that can see your opponents movement not in real time but in slow motion.

How does this work in Acting? How do know you when you've tapped into your sub-conscious? In Acting there is a phrase, "I felt like I was flying onstage."

The **State of Flying** for the actor is walking off stage and not remembering anything that happened in your performance. However, you'll never forget that feeling of Flying.

To tap into the sub-conscious, we must have a conscious contact with our muscle memory, and to achieve this we must know that:

1) Repetition is the key to open the pathway.

2) Breath is the key to pathway.

3) The breath flows toward the center of the body. The center of the body is the key to the pathway.

4) To locate your center, focus on your belly button, and imagine an inch below your belly button is the place where lies your center. Now breathe into that place.

The Zen Artist

I was watching a documentary on an Artist and his process.

He described his approach to his work. He would lay out his brushes and paints in system around himself, like a drummer with their skins, exactly where he needed them to be. He then attached a very expensive canvas to his easel. He would then sit, and reach for a brush, aim that brush at color but never touch the paint. He would flash the dry brush across the canvas, he would do this day after day, hour after hour, not counting, not thinking, until one day the brush would hit a color and he was painting. The process allowed him to let go of the limited conscious mind to tap into the vast sub-conscious.

Thoughts

MANTRA #4.

Acting is a simple craft for complicated people.

Always Leave Some Blood On The Floor.

(Figuratively, if not literally)

Today in your class or rehearsal:

Did you push yourself as far as you could?
Did you dig deep or were you holding back? Do you want
to be an actor who gives, or the actor who talks about it?
Are you performing in your head?

MANTRA # 5

Live Violently In Your Art, To Be Serene In Your Life.

Rehearsal Notes #2.

If the Director hasn't given you a note, don't ask, "Why haven't you given me a note?"

Because that's the best note you'll get.

During note sessions always listen, even if that note doesn't apply to you, because all notes apply to you.

Thoughts

MANTRA #6

Always Make The Stupid Choice.

The stupid choice being the first one that comes into your head before the Board of Directors in charge of your insecurity start to whisper *"That's a stupid choice, that's a stupid choice."*

The actor's first choice is the purest, it's unfiltered and undiluted. No matter what, always go with the "Stupid Choice." Trust creative self, not your critical self.

Rehearsal Notes #3

If you leave a rehearsal feeling terrible about your work, it was probably a good rehearsal as the actor isn't a good judge of their own work. The actor's job is to do the work, not judge their work.

What seems to be getting in your way during rehearsal?
Are you working to please the director?
Are you trying to please the room?
Are you performing in your head and not in the moment with the other actors?

How to get out of your own way in rehearsal:
You must be willing to create work that is fearless.
You must be willing to risk never working with this director again.
It is none of your business what other actors think about your work.
As an actor, you're not here to seek approval or make other actors happy.

Rehearsal isn't a popularity contest.
An actor has to have a strong sense of self:
We listen, we are generous, engaged, compassionate, helpful to all in rehearsal, but we don't betray ourselves and our work to make others more comfortable.
Don't be a people pleaser, as that is the worst thing that an actor can be.

Are You a People Pleaser?

MANTRA #7

"Don't Be Afraid To Be A Rotten Actor."

-Andre Belgrader, Director, Teacher.

Dennis Hilton-Reid

Thoughts

Fun.

FUN: enjoyment, amusement, or lighthearted pleasure.
As an actor when I was told to have fun, it always sounded disingenuous - that my work was frivolous. Yes, I am in the entertainment industry, the story telling business, to amuse, for people to enjoy, for pleasure.

Shakespeare wrote his plays to entertain but also to reflect what we as human beings experience no matter what station in life. That's what a story teller does – reflect what is seen - and an actor interprets what is written into their imagination by transforming their ideas, experiences and observations into living breathing organic beings. Whether it's the Lover, Queen murderess, rapist Prince, thief Count, genial Baker, proud Prostitute, scared King, reluctant Princess, racist Judge. The actor searches for the characters inner truth, and for their own empathy to not judge, which is the pure part of any science from chemistry, physics to law and medicine.

The meaning of "To have fun" changed for me when I understood the job in hand and the nature of what I was doing and why I was doing it. There is a reason why Arts and Sciences are folded together - simply put, exploration.

So, "To Have Fun" is to be engaged with commitment, honesty, boldness, truth, daring and exploration. If you're engaged in any of these in pursuit of doing great work, the audience will be as engaged with supporting you on the mutual journey that is being shared. Simply put, they will have fun as they watch you have serious fun.

MANTRA #8.

Are You a People Pleaser in Your Work?

The only person the actor should please, is themself.

An Actor Never Asks For Permission?

Do you ask the Casting Director or Director if you can use a chair when you walk into an audition?

Do you ask the Director if you can use a prop when you're in rehearsal or if you start on the floor when you're in class?

A painter never asks for permission to use a color; if the photographer asks permission to take the shot it's gone forever; the musician never stops in the middle of a solo to ask the other band members for permission to play a chord.

Why then do actors feel the need to ask for permission?

Asking for permission, getting the OK, seeking approval, is just another way of stopping impulses, halting the flow of playing off your partner. Asking for permission is to open the sluice gates of the fear of "being wrong" and "doing it wrong" to gush through and take over.

Remember - if the Director doesn't like your choice they'll tell you.

Your job is to do, to create, to not think, to act.

act: verb

take action, take steps, take measures, move, react.

MANTRA #9

The only person in my way is me...I must get out of my own way.

Are You Waiting to Call Yourself An Actor?

(No one has the right to tell you that you're not an Actor) When do you say yes! I'm an actor! When you get your first check? SAG card? Join Equity? Your first Union Job? Or is it the first time you step into an acting class, voice class or a speech class.

I had spent years jumping from job to job until finally at the age of 19 I landed in a company working as a junior design engineer. It was a great company, good people, I learned a lot, they paid for me to go to school, they were encouraging and supportive, but I wasn't happy. I felt out of place and I never felt like a designer, so I never referred to myself as one. Eventually I left that company, got on a flight and came to NY. I fell in love in NYC and wanted to stay. One day I was walking down Madison Avenue and saw the American Academy of Dramatic Arts, I had no intention of becoming an actor, I walked in and decided to audition.

A year later, when I came back to NYC for good as a student at the Academy, I sat in my first class - a speech class - and felt at home, I never felt more comfortable and connected as I did in that moment and in that moment I knew that I was in the right place. In that moment I became an actor, because I knew that's who I had always been, I just had to find it.

Does a writer wait for the first novel to be published to call themselves a writer?

You're either a dancer or you're not, you're either a musician or not, you're either a painter or you're not.

You're either an Actor or you're not...no one can tell you either way...it's up to you.

MANTRA #10

"I Must Not Be Afraid Of Going Into The Fight."

-Anon

Whose Rules?

Rules. My rules? Her rules? His rules? Whose rules? Why is it that actors always seem to have a set of rules with no handbook and no idea where they come from?

There are no rules, only routines: warm up, be present, learn lines, go over staging, get focused and establish a routine: Routine is discipline.

However routine and discipline are not the same as superstition, which is prevalent amongst actors; e.g. I must sit at the last chair in the dressing room with my left side near the back door and my head tilted forward at a 13 degree angle to the mirror with only six lights on and not twelve I cannot enter the Theatre laughing because I only said Strindberg's name five times instead of six in the last rehearsal.

Yes the plague of the superstition that can make or break, hold sway over and deign a performance as doomed. It's not productive to invest in hooey-fun, but dangerous.

Don't give your power away to fallacy.

Tradition is not Superstition: saying ~~Macbeth~~ "The Scottish Play" in a rehearsal is a great Theatrical tradition - as whistling in the Theatre is considered bad luck.
Traditions are what bond all of us to the same institution, it's our belief system, our code, our language, our culture.
Traditions are community.
Discipline is absolute.
Superstitions are fickle.

Thoughts

MANTRA #11

Am I Teachable?

Today I Will Be Teachable.

Are You a Worker Amongst Workers?

No, this isn't some humdrum Marxist axiom.
A worker amongst workers is being humble and a part of the group, whether you're playing Cleopatra or first guard from the left.

Being a professional just means being supportive to everyone whether you like them or not, not gossiping about the production, fellow actors, the Director, the costumes, the sets, the script or how clean or big the rehearsal space is.

Just be a Worker Amongst Workers.

MANTRA # 12

My Ego Is In My Way.

Let Go of My Ego, and Let My Gift Shine Through.

Are You Fighting Your Director In Your Head?

If you are, it's losing fight. If you are, you're being passive aggressive. If you are, you're being controlling and if you are, you're hurting yourself more than them.

If you don't know how to communicate what you want from your teacher or director, how can you communicate your character to the audience?

If you don't understand a note, then say so.

If you're not getting what you think you need, then ask.

If you're struggling with the work, then say so.

No one is a mind reader. It's your responsibility to take care of your creative needs.

MANTRA # 13

I Am Responsible For Me.

Once Through The Door.

As soon as you step through the door to the rehearsal studio, you must be in work mode. How to do that when you want to settle in, drink your beverage, nibble on a snack, chit-chat to your mates about what's going on after rehearsal or gossip about…stuff? And before you know it, rehearsal has become hang out, has become a leisure activity, has become resistance to doing anything other than avoiding the work.

As actors, we have to go places that we sometimes don't want to. It's not that we are lazy, it's more that "I'm not in the mood to go there."

There lies the dilemma, how to get in the mood. As soon as you step though the door run these words through your mind: Happy, Glad, Sad, Mad or Afraid. Then choose one with out thinking, say it out loud, then go from there. You have expressed your true feeling and now it's out. You can do this with as many partners as possible.

It's not about your mood, it comes down to your preparation and being ready.

MANTRA #14

Am I in My Head?

I must get out of my Head.

Engage Your Imagination:

What were your immediate images and thoughts when you first read the script? Was your imagination bursting with an overflow of ideas? Were you excited about the first rehearsal? And then you put the script down and Crash! each one of these great thoughts is sliced and diced by negativity, and once again our old friend Fear rules and dominates your creativity.

What to do?

Write down your thoughts and ideas on a notepad as you read the script, thereby keeping your ideas intact while allowing a fluid stream of connectivity from your imagination stream free fresh, raw, images intact. Writing your ideas down you gives them credibility, so that the next time you read the script you can go back into it that place and engage your imagination in a deeper way by following the same method. Getting the first round out of your head allows new images, ideas, thoughts to enter which are deeper.

By doing this your ideas become a plan of action, fear is abated, self-doubt is shredded, creative balance is restored.

That is why you Always Engage Your Imagination.

Dennis Hilton-Reid

Thoughts

MANTRA #14

A Clean Script is An Unloved Script.

A Dirty Script Is a Loved Script.

(mark it, write on it, dog ear it, fold it back, crease it. Coffee stains allowed.)

What's On Your Nightstand?

What books are you reading?

Are you reading anything other than a play?

Books help with keeping your mind active in thoughts and ideas of another world. More importantly - language.

Read novels, biographies, memoirs, non-fiction.
For it's important that actors read so that your mind is engaged in language, information and education. The actor's world cannot be reduced to just the theatre.

MANTRA #15

To tell the worlds' stories, I must read those stories.

The Actors Three Musts.

1. Direct a play or a scene.

Why?

- Directing is the skill of moving the vision of the production forward from all points from design to text analysis to working with actors. It's the Art of Collaboration.

What does the Actor take from Directing?

- Listening.
- The Bigger Picture.
- How to Tell a Story.

2. Singing before an audience.

Why?

- Vulnerability.
- Channeling Fear.

3. Stand Up Comedy.

Why?

- Being present.
- No safety net.
- Thinking on your feet.

MANTRA #16

Let Go Into The Nothingness.

Dennis Hilton-Reid

Thoughts

Don't Cheat Yourself.

Have you found your rehearsal clique?
When you go to class do you only hang with your "people"?
Do you sit next to your people and whisper to them during class?
Do you have shared private "in-jokes" that no one else understands?
Do you also have a constant running dialogue, flow of eye-rolls, lip reading and body shrugs while others are working with your people?

If so, you are either an energy sucker, or a focus thief. Which one are you? If this is you then maybe you're in the wrong business, because that behavior says more about you than the person you're mocking or ignoring.

An actor takes interest in all of their peers. No one should be ostracized in the studio, or rehearsal space.

The actor should relish the opportunity to learn from their peers, how they work, warm up, rehearse.

We support each other, if you can't there are plenty of careers where you can be a narcissist.

If you're generous of spirit, you will be trusted by your peers.

We don't have to like the people we work with, but we have to work with them.

Be of service to the production.

MANTRA #17

"Don't Quit Before The First Ten Years."

-Dennis Moore, acting teacher and director

Stuck: Remember You Have A Tool Box.

Are you in the trap of the "What Now's?" because "Nothing's Working"? or "I'm Feeling Lost"?

Are you using your toolbox?

Improvise the scene.

Swap roles.

Do you need more relaxation?

Sit in a chair and breathe, let the mind go and focus on the character and connect them to the world they are in.

Find your characters breath:
How do they breathe? Deep, shallow, fast, slow, labored, panicked?
Place: What is the place, time, day, month and season that you're in? Be specific.

Go back to the basics…they will never let you down.

> Don't bring your process into rehearsal. Be a professional, bring the work.

MANTRA # 18

Chase your fear, don't let your fear chase you.

Thoughts

STAGE FRIGHT-PERFORMANCE FRIGHT: AKA THE FEAR OF ACTING

The question is, does this have more to do with who's out there than your preparedness? Are you prepared?

If your worried about a friend, a spouse, a potential love watching your work when you come on stage, then you're focused on the wrong thing. Everyone wants you to do well, but you can't do well if you're in your head monitoring your performance for the audience and the special members that have come to see you, family, friends, agents and managers alike. Just do what you've been doing for the rehearsal period, focus on the energy of your partner, keep the focus on whoever you're performing with, keeping in mind to be conscious of the audience but not being subservient to them.

Film has other demands when it comes to your work and performance fright. You have to make the camera your friend, not the crew, you can't want to satisfy the director but rather use all the energy that's being focused on you toward your performance.

Concentration is the key and staying with that inner life that you have created. And if none of that is working then do what Laurence Olivier would do.

To be nervous is a part of the hi-wire act that is acting-acknowledge and accept.

If you're not nervous, then something is wrong-you may have shut down all feeling and that you do not want. So stay nervously energized, change nervous to excited, transform those nerves into energy. And if all else fails do what Lawrence Olivier would do:

"Olivier would regularly stand backstage, saying of his audience: "You bastards!""

MANTRA # 19

Do I Want To Be An Actor?

I am an Actor.

Act As If.

LISTENING.

Are you truly listening?

I mean truly, clearly, with full commitment? Are you listening to the other actors around while working?

Are you listening with your eyes, nose, mouth, gut, back, groin. Are you listening?

Or are you in and out of the moment?

Listening is the skill, what you do with what you hear is the talent.

Are You Listening?

MANTRA # 20

Help me to listen

DON'T PLAY WHAT'S THERE, PLAY WHAT ISN'T THERE. - *MILES DAVIS*

So what does this have to do with acting? Miles's advice is clearly geared to musicians, or is it?

A script has details, and these details are hidden within the language, not only in the stage directions, but between the lines.

The lines that are given by the actor to another actor are a road map to engage your imagination truthfully. Work toward what the text asks you to do not in the obvious way. Play against the obvious immediate reading of the text; for example if the character has pages of dialogue that are angry, try the opposite. This will give you internal conflict. Try laughing for as long as you can even if it doesn't read that the character would do that...try it! Read the happy character with anger, the stupid with guile, the courageous with fear. This is where the actor can play what isn't there.

It may not be on the page, but take the chance and "Play what isn't there".

MANTRA # 21

Run into the terror.

prejudice | ˈprejədəs | ***noun***
preconceived opinion that is not based on reason or
actual experience:
DO YOU QUESTION THE EXPERIENCE
BEFORE HAVING THE EXPERIENCE?

This the duality of defense and action.
When you are asked to make an adjustment or try an
improvisation by your Director or teacher to gain further
insight, do you engage in asking the question "Why?" and
other tactics to avoid? If so, then you're devaluing your
experience and valuing safety over creative risk.

As an actor, everything you discover, whether in the studio
or the rehearsal room, affects everyone else's process. You
are a part of, not separate from, the whole. Your work may
affect another actor that isn't in a scene with you, it may
inform the cast, help your classmates, open up the
production, inspire the director.

So, when you stop to talk about the experience you are
about to have, you are impeding the free flow of creativity.
Go, take a chance, and then talk about it after, because
then you are talking from an informed place.

The Artist who questions the event never taken is just a
spectator waiting until it's safe.

Don't tell me your opinion on the world if you've never
left your village.

To be an Actor, make sure your priorities are in order.

Act for the JOY of it.

Thoughts

To be an Actor, make sure your priorities are in order.

Act for the **GLORY** of it.

As an actor, I don't want positive reinforcement about a lack of self esteem, I want Mantras that capture my "Want" and that want is to dig deeper into my soul.

Mantras that guide me on my relentless "Search" for honesty and truth in my work, which at times can feel oblique, evasive. The Search for the Invisible City, the Golden Kingdom, Atlantis is fueled with desire, drive and belief. Above all an actor has to posses a strong sense of self, without the concepts such as "Want" and "Search" are just that…concepts

Dennis Hilton-Reid

Thoughts

To be an Actor, make sure your priorities are in order

To Be of Service.

Do I want to be seen?

Stop waiting for your dreams to come true, they have...you're an Actor...now just do the work.

ABOUT THE AUTHOR

Dennis Hilton-Reid lives in New York City and has worked both in the US and internationally as a theatre artist for over 30 years.

He has taught at Fordham University, Vassar College, SUNY Purchase, NYU, Stella Adler, the American Musical and Dramatic Academy and the American Academy of Dramatic Arts. His acting workshops have been presented both domestically and abroad.

He was awarded a Jerome Fellowship for his one-man show "Mandingo of Manhattan," as a resident artist at the Mabou Mines suite.

As an actor he has performed at Cidermill Playhouse; Cincinnati Playhouse in the Park, Guthrie, Kennedy Center, Yale Rep; Voice and Vision, Rites and Reason, HERE, NADA, the Public Theater, CSC, La Mama, Ohio Theater, En Garde Arts, and the Spoleto Festival.

He has directed over forty productions in educational and professional theaters in the US and internationally.

He is a graduate of Yale University and a member of the Actors Studio PDU.

Made in the USA
Middletown, DE
24 November 2021

52543493R00050